MERITOCRACY AND THE 'CLASSLESS SOCIETY'
by Adrian Wooldridge

The Social Market Foundation
1995

First published in May 1995
by
The Social Market Foundation
20, Queen Anne's Gate
London SW1H 9AA
Tel: 0171-222 7060 Fax: 0171-222 0310

Paper No. 21

ISBN 1 874097 70 4

Cover design by Adrian Taylor

Printed in Great Britain by
Xenogamy plc
Suite 2, Westcombe House
7-9 Stafford Road, Wallington, Surrey SM6 9AN
Typesetting by Wimyk Enterprises

CONTENTS

THE AUTHOR

ADRIAN WOOLDRIDGE is a Fellow of All Souls College, Oxford and a journalist with the *Economist*. His *Measuring the Mind. Education and Psychology in England c.1860-1990* was published last year by Cambridge University Press.

ACKNOWLEDGEMENTS

I am grateful to Daniel Finkelstein for suggesting that I write this pamphlet and for his helpful comments on his first draft, and to Roderick Nye for his excellent editing. Responsibility for errors or infelicities is mine alone.

Foreword

After 30 years or more in the social policy wilderness, the idea that there is such a thing as innate ability and that developing it should be the primary aim of governments remains a controversial one.

A serious discussion about the merits of meritocracy is often clouded by charges of elitism, callousness, or worse; the recent publication of Charles Murray's and Richard Herrnstein's *The Bell Curve* has unleashed a barrage of criticism from those who wish to ignore individual differences in intellectual abilities.

The reason for this is understandable. Entrenched interests have grown up around policies which favour group entitlements over individual merits and which place the cohesion of communities above personal choice. These same voices continue to dominate the debate over the future of the welfare state, even as the measures they champion are shown to have produced a society which is in many ways more fragmented and unequal than ever.

Set against this background Adrian Wooldridge has written a paper which explains why merit matters both for the future economic prosperity of Britain and its continuing social stability. Rather than harking back to a golden age that never was or looking forward to a society based on equal outcomes which can never be, he argues for a fairer and more efficient opportunity state based on the values of competition, choice and personal responsibility.

Developing innate talent is above all a moral pursuit, one from which we can derive constant values in a changing world. Designing social policies from education to social security which recognise and cater to individual differences should therefore be a matter of urgency across the political spectrum, Wooldridge says.

As such his paper deserves to be read by all those with an interest in the respective roles of the individual, communities and the state in a modern society.

Roderick Nye
May 1995

Chapter 1: Introduction: Why Merit Matters

Meritocracy and markets

The defining achievement of the 1980s was not so much material as intellectual: the revival, after decades of neglect, of belief in the market. This revival did not just take the obvious, if startling, forms of the collapse of central planning in the East, the privatisation of state-owned industries in the West, the exhaustion of the 'middle way' in Scandinavia. It also involved humbler, but still hard-fought changes: the introduction of the price mechanism into the welfare state in Britain, New Zealand and a handful of other pioneers and, perhaps more unexpected still, the restructuring of giant corporations on full-blooded market principles, with the spread of delayering, contracting out, performance-related pay, market testing and the like.

The most pressing task for the rest of the 1990s is to revive another Enlightenment ideal which has fallen out of favour in the last few decades, that of meritocracy. The meritocratic ideal combines three virtues which ought to be at the heart of any successful economy. It advances social justice, by allocating jobs to the able rather than the well-connected; promotes economic efficiency, by ensuring that round pegs are placed in round holes; and diminishes bigotry, by treating people as individuals, not just as representatives of social groups. By uprooting vested interests, it unleashes economic energies; by abolishing patronage, it institutionalises self-reliance; and by rewarding intellectual success, it encourages educational effort. It is thus the key to creating not only a more efficient society, but also a more moral and enlightened one.

Calling for the revival of meritocracy sounds rather like calling for a revival of motherhood and apple pie. Surely we all believe that opportunities should be awarded on the basis of abilities rather than connections? Francis Fukuyama, for example, argues that, now that history has come to an end, we have nothing but a timeless meritocracy to look forward to. In the past, he says, people and nations were differentiated from each other by a host of artificial barriers. The end of history, that is the victory of liberal principles, has wiped away many of those man-made barriers. This has not ended stratification, but has rather put it on a different basis. Enhanced equality of opportunity in liberal states has levelled the paying field in critical respects, but sharpened social inequality in other ways by allowing educated and skilled people to rise to the top in a technologically-stratified meritocracy.[1]

In other words, we are all meritocrats now.

Meritocracy under siege

Alas, he is wrong. In the 1950s and 1960s policy makers turned against meritocracy in favour of two very different principles: equality and community. Egalitarians advanced three arguments against meritocracy: that all forms of social selection are notoriously fallible; that a decent society ought to aim at equality of outcome rather than equality of opportunity; and that individual differences are the result of social background rather than innate abilities, so that promoting people on the basis of 'merit' is tantamount to rewarding them for coming from 'good' families. In advancing these arguments they quoted the authority of a growing number of sociologists and sociologically-minded psychologists.

Some communitarians were even more uncompromising. They argued that a meritocratic society would be even more repulsive than the class-stratified society which it was intended to replace, promoting intolerable smugness on the part of the winners, who would believe that they deserved all they got, and unbearable alienation on the part of the losers, who would have nobody to blame for their failure but themselves.

The egalitarian tradition has received rapturous support from the both sides of the Atlantic. American liberals have reversed what was once their most heartfelt belief: that people should be judged according to the content of their characters rather than the colour of their skins or the configuration of their genitalia. Many Americans now think of themselves not as responsible individuals, capable of fashioning their own fates, but as representatives of oppressed groups, petitioning politicians for entitlements.

While all this was going on, the right did too little to sustain the meritocratic principle. Traditionalists in the UK concentrated on defending old-fashioned grammar schools and the established curriculum, rather than acknowledging the shortcomings of a selective system of education which failed to reflect the full range of abilities in the population, and did little to engage the interests and stretch the minds of non-academic children. Free marketers were content to invoke the magic of the market. They wanted to shrink the state, not reform it; to hand decision-making to parents, through vouchers, not to equalise educational opportunities or refine educational selection.

Thanks to the moral certainties of the left and the intellectual woolliness of the right, egalitarian arguments have had a dramatic impact on social policy. Visit many schools in England and the atmosphere is that of a holiday camp, anarchic and unstructured, with everything done to indulge the children's fragile feelings of self-worth. The Americans have gone even further and institutionalised a gigantic system of affirmative action, based on the idea that an officially-certificated clique of patrons should allocate opportunities on the basis of group membership.

Little happened in the 1980s to undo the damage. While Margaret Thatcher sought to shake Britain free of its sentimental attachment to equality and community, she turned to education too late in her premiership to undermine the comprehensive principle in state schools. And though John Major once spoke tantalisingly about his belief in a 'classless society', he has failed to flesh out his vision or drive through a coherent meritocratic agenda.

One reason why politicians have been so hesitant to promote meritocracy is that it is far from being all motherhood and apple pie. The post-War critics of the idea, from Michael Young onwards, may have exaggerated their case, but they understood that meritocracy is a demanding taskmaster, not a helping of saccharine. It brings the disadvantages of competition as well as the upsides, the pains of downward mobility as well as the joys of success. The rewards of a new meritocratic revolution will be high, but the fighting will not be easy nor the results instantaneous.

But then again reviving the free-market ideal was not easy, either. Meritocrats need to imitate free-marketeers by concentrating, to start with, on the battle of ideas. The best way to prepare for this battle is to turn to the past; to remind ourselves of just how heroic a part the meritocratic ideal has played in British history and of how high a price we have paid for rejecting that idea.

Chapter 2: The Rise and Fall of Meritocracy

The rise of meritocracy

The meritocratic ideal in Britain was first turned from a philosophical debating point into a dynamic political creed by the 'intellectual aristocracy' — a powerful connection of intermarried families, including the Huxleys, the Darwins and the Wedgwoods, who owed their pre-eminence to their intellect and education and who hoped to advance their social position by abolishing patronage and throwing opportunities open to talent to create a natural ruling class.[2]

The intellectual aristocracy's most articulate spokesman was the historian Thomas Macaulay who put forward three ideas which would become central the meritocratic ideal: that men differ in their inborn 'talents' and 'diligence'; that inborn ability is not quite the same thing as 'mere learning'; and that examinations, by detecting these underlying powers of mind, can predict 'what men will prove to be in life'.[3]

A large chunk of British society after the mid-19th century was reconstructed on this basis. The Northcote-Trevelyan reforms replaced recruitment by patronage in the Civil Service with competitive examinations. Similarly the Government forced Oxford and Cambridge to do away with 'closed' fellowships and to start awarding academic positions on the basis of merit.

To accompany these changes at the top, Victorian society built a scholarship ladder stretching from the slums to Oxbridge, which was intended to take able children, regardless of their backgrounds, to the educations and careers for which their talents marked them out. But meritocracy was more than just a means for improving public service, replacing the dull and idle with the able and energetic; it was also a moral crusade. Competition would promote self-reliance and other such vigorous virtues, transforming offices from freeholds, earned by flattery, into trusts, awarded for merit.[4] It would also reinvigorate English education, encouraging parents to send their children to school and the children, once there, to persevere with their studies.

So persuasive were the moral as well as practical arguments for meritocracy, that what had begun as a Whig policy was supported by socialists such as Sidney Webb and RH Tawney. They sought to broaden the ladder of opportunity and to strengthen its rungs, so that jobs went to those who truly deserved them, but few questioned the underlying premises of the meritocratic ideal.

That ideal reached its apotheosis in the post-War tripartite education system, outlined by the Conservative, RA Butler, in his 1944 Education Act and lovingly constructed by Clement Attlee's Labour government. The system had its weaknesses largely as a result of the failure to build the third leg of the tripod, technical education. But it was motivated by a noble aim, supported across the political spectrum, to ensure that the education system was stratified on the basis of intellectual capacity rather than social class. The Education Act transformed grammar schools by forcing them to recruit pupils from a wider section of society and by providing the chosen ones, including Mrs Thatcher and many of her leading disciples, with a highly efficient escalator into the universities and the elite.[5]

The sins of the meritocrats
This largely Victorian version of meritocracy yielded some extraordinary results. It transformed Oxford and Cambridge into two of the most successful universities in the world; created a civil service capable of running a world-spanning Empire; and produced a political elite capable of coming to terms with the rise of mass politics.

But meritocracy, Victorian-style, also bred divisions among meritocrats themselves. The professional elite turned against the business class and used the universities, the civil service and the public schools to promote the virtues of public service over the evils of money-making. The result was that the meritocracy suffered from three fatal flaws.

The first was its general bias against utility, and individualist capitalism in particular. The reformed universities and public schools concentrated on teaching the classics and instilling gentlemanly virtues; their ideal products did not necessarily own any land, but they were landowners in the eyes of God.[6] The ladder of merit increased the range of candidates for elite positions without challenging this dominant ideal: the grammar schools competed with the public schools but hoped to produce the same product. Even the Workers Educational Association was infused with the spirit of Rugby and Balliol, thanks to the tireless work of RH Tawney. This tradition looked down on anything which smacked of the practical world. ('One would really think it was a crime to aim at the material happiness of the human race,' complained one critic of the time, Dean Farrar.[7])

Victorian meritocracy's second flaw was its unimaginative elitism. Many meritocrats thought that the function of education was 'to rake a few geniuses up from the rubbish' (to borrow a phrase from Thomas Jefferson). They put a disproportionate amount of effort into discovering, nurturing and comforting the chosen few but failed to think hard about constructing a proper educational system for the mass of the population. They allowed their obsession with grammar schools to distract them from building a proper system of technical education. Above all, the meritocrats only had a one-dimensional view of merit. They identified all merit with academic ability and assumed that all abilities are interrelated, so that an able historian might easily have become an able mathematician, had he only had the inclination.

The third weakness was an unworldliness which comes from job security. The intellectual aristocrats who wrested control of the civil service and the universities in the mid-nineteenth century, were not interested in abolishing tenure, but simply in transferring it from the landed elite to themselves. Meritocrats have traditionally glided through a series of inward-looking institutions, cloistered and cosseted, without allowing the messy modern world to intrude. Dons have never had to face the struggle for tenure which is routine in American universities. Fast stream civil servants are on an upward escalator for life.

The result of these flaws was that meritocracy came to be seen as increasingly outdated and divisive. It did not serve all classes as it should, it failed to equip Britons to meet the challenges of the post-War world, and it had simply replaced one self-perpetuating elite with another. Given that the meritocrats could not even agree among themselves, they were scarcely well-placed to face the attack on the entire ideal when it came.

Insulting intelligence testing

If the 1944 Education Act was the high water mark of meritocracy, it was followed depressingly quickly by an anti-meritocatic backlash. What began with a questioning of the '11+' tests which were used to decide which children went to grammar schools, soon developed into a full-scale assault on the idea that innate, general cognitive ability could be defined and measured reliably through any form of intelligence tests.

The rise of psychometry and that of meritocracy had gone hand in hand. Psychometrists believed in the inevitability of social mobility. Cyril Burt, the most influential advocate of IQ testing during its golden age and a fervent supporter of the 1945 Labour government, calculated that in order for people to do the jobs they were suited to by ability, almost a quarter of children would have to end up in different social classes from their parents.

IQ testers were often the most radical of meritocrats and passionate 'modernists'. They believed that if Britain were to have any chance of surviving as a serious country, it needed to put much more emphasis on teaching science. One of their greatest disappointments was that Butler succeeded in protecting the traditional grammar school curriculum, with its obsession with literary and classical education, from reform in 1944.

They were advocates for spending money on the welfare state in general, and public education in particular, arguing for raising the school-leaving age, improved teacher-training, increasing the number of nursery schools, and regular medical inspection of school children. Ironically, as it turned out, IQ testers also tended to be enthusiastic, arguably over-enthusiastic, devotees of child-centred education. Alfred Binet invented IQ tests to identify backward children, who were having a miserable time trying to keep up with more able contemporaries. And Cyril Burt, in one of his most eloquent and sympathetic books, *The Backward Child*, argued that, because the backward differ so much among themselves, they require smaller classes, individual attention, and scope to express their own abilities and aptitudes.

None of this was to save psychometrists from the attack unleashed on the premisses and practices of their profession. Biologists like Lancelot Hogben argued that ability was the result of a complex interaction between nature and nurture and that this mix varied from child to child. Sociologists like RM Titmuss worried that working-class children were loosing out in the race for grammar school places and speculated that IQ might owe more to social circumstances like poor nutrition and bad housing than to cognitive abilities. Psychologists noted that coaching and practice raised children's average test scores, suggesting that selection and streaming were self-fulfilling prophesies. Further studies argued that the tests themselves were unreliable not only because they failed to measure the same quality in the same way on different occasions, but also because the quality measured itself altered and that mental growth, like physical growth, comes in spurts.

The coming of comprehensives
From around 1960 criticism of British meritocracy grew more harsh. A series of Government-sponsored reports suggested that meritocratic selection failed to

address the social factors behind the under-achievement of poor pupils. Alongside these sociological objections, were raised new cultural ones. Selection debilitated communities because it alienated bright, but poor, children from their roots, it was said. Grammar schools were condemned as a breeding ground for dull uniformity and deference. Not only did meritocracy not work in practice, it was now also wrong in principle. Faced with this onslaught, the political consensus which had sustained the meritocratic ideal for almost a century began to unravel.

Labour intellectuals had already begun to fall out of love with meritocracy because it perpetuated sharp inequalities of wealth and power rather than promoting equality of outcome. Added to this there was widespread popular anxiety about the all-or-nothing nature of the examinations taken at the age of 11. The '11+' allocated children irrevocably between grammar schools with high reputations and established links to the universities and the professions; and secondary modern schools with low reputations which fed their pupils into working-class jobs.

Tony Crosland, the future Secretary of State for Education, relied heavily on both the egalitarian and the communitarian cases against meritocracy in his long campaign to establish education 'as a serious alternative to nationalisation in promoting a more just and efficient society'.[8] He made it clear that equality of opportunity was only one stage on the road to equality of outcome. By itself it promoted 'insecurity and ferocious competition'; threatened to 'replace one remote elite (based on lineage) by a new one (based on ability and intelligence)'; and induced a total sense of inferiority in those who failed, since they could no longer blame the system.[9] He hoped instead to create a new system, that of a common education which would be the harbinger of a common culture and an egalitarian society. Thus the policy of comprehensive schools was born.

From merits to entitlements
Though education was the main British battleground, it was by no means the only terrain on which the anti-meritocrats fought on either side of the Atlantic. During the 1960s and 1970s they discovered that building an egalitarian society involved more than just abolishing academic selection. The introduction of mixed ability classes, informal teaching and the development of curricula less centred on middle class values was only part of a wider revolt against every sort of classification and boundary.

These divided individuals from one another rather than celebrating their common humanity; they perpetuated the idea that some types of behaviour were more 'normal' and 'respectable' than others; and they implied that the price of civilisation is the control of feelings and the suppression of desires. The intellectual avant garde of the 1960s — Michael Foucault and RD Laing, Herbert Marcuse and Norman O Brown — specialised in the subversion of received categories. Their main target for subversion was the idea that the individual is a distinctive agent, endowed with a mind, a will and a moral responsibility for his actions.

It was not merely this rejection of individualism which undermined meritocracy, by making it inappropriate. The apparent abundance of the age, also rendered it unnecessary as a just, if austere, means of allocating scarce opportunities. The meritocratic ideal rewarded self-denial and punished self-indulgence. However under a regime of plenty, egalitarians argued that such a disciplined rationing of opportunities was plainly outdated. Brian Jackson voiced the hopes of a generation:

> Our society is one of opportunity and possibly plenty. We reduce its potentialities by an educational sieve designed for a society of scarcity. In the past the sieve served well enough.... It was not just, but it was the nearest to justice that circumstances allowed. Today it's absurd. It limits us, occupying our attention with the tiny details that divide and label us -draining our energies away from the colossal opportunities for human development that our wealth and knowledge promise.[10]

It was the insistence of left-wing movements that virtue was a property not of individuals but of categories, twinned with the idea that there was enough opportunity for everyone if only power and wealth were shared equally which finally marginalised the meritocratic tradition. The triumph of interest-group politics, born out of the collective struggle for the rights of 'oppressed groups' such as women, blacks, workers, or students, was made both possible and necessary by an ever-expanding and ambitious state which sought to plan production and micro-manage society. This revolution in the rules which governed the distribution of rewards had a huge impact on individual behaviour. People sought advance not through evident achievement but through political agitation. As a result, inequalities grew wider and society more polarised than ever.

Against equality

It was of course supposed to be different. A policy of entitlements based on equality and community summons up the vision of a world in which everybody has a decent share of the good things in life, in which neighbours go our of their way to help neighbours, in which the streets are clean and parent-association meetings are packed: a world that is far removed from the rubbish-strewn estates and asocial teenagers of modern Britain, or the urban slums where the American underclass congregates.

The reasons for this disparity between theory and practice are not hard to divine. Egalitarian policies have a habit of being self-defeating. While selective schools extracted able working-class children from their local communities and forced them to mix with their equally able middle-class peers, comprehensive schools have replaced selection by ability with selection by house price. Even within the same city or town middle-class children go to middle-class comprehensives, which usually boast good teachers and decent facilities, while working-class children make do with working-class comprehensives, which struggle with worse teachers and shoddier facilities. When they do attend the same school, children from different social classes have usually operated a policy of self-segregation, with middle-class children congregating in the top classes and working-class children, however bright, falling to the bottom.

The failure of radical egalitarian educational reform is not peculiar to Britain. President Johnson's 'unconditional war on poverty' unleashed a 30 year phase of lavish Federal expenditure on compensatory education for the disadvantaged — and in particular for ethnic minorities — which failed to break the cycle of poverty. Moves to equalise funding between schools in black and white areas did not result in an equalisation of academic results. Attempts to produce more racially integrated schools often produced the opposite result, as white urbanites, terrified of forced integration, upped sticks and moved to the suburbs. As early as 1972 Christopher Jencks's classic study, *Inequality*, acknowledged the demise of educational optimism and argued that on the basis of a mass of evidence that educational reform had done little to solve social inequalities.[11] That impression was reinforced by the unchanging social composition of the elite, which the vast expansion of educational institutions in the 1950s and 1960s failed to alter. It led one of the leading British egalitarians, AH Halsey, to conclude that 'the essential fact of twentieth century educational history is that egalitarian policies have failed'.[12]

In general, the state is remarkably bad at promoting equality. The fact that something is publicly provided does not mean that everyone will get equal access to it. The middle classes do much better than the working classes out of the welfare state, from the way they use the National Health Service to taking their pick of university places.[13]

Not that this has stopped governments from attempting ever more extreme measures in pursuit of equality. Egalitarian social policy reached its nadir with positive discrimination, or affirmative action. Affirmative action replaces self-help with patronage, transforming university officials into surly patrons, bent on reshaping institutions according to passing fashions, and potential students into clients, forced to tout for places on the basis of their ethnic or sexual characteristics. Group-based discrimination is a remarkably crude way of helping the disadvantaged. Not all minorities are regarded as equally worthy of affirmative action; orientals for example have to get a higher score than both blacks and whites. Nor is affirmative action likely to reach those blacks who are in most need of government help. Throughout the era of affirmative action the poorest blacks have been losing ground against the rest of society.

Against community
If egalitarian social policies have failed to promote the equality of outcome that they were designed to deliver, they have also failed to secure what John Major famously described as 'a nation at ease with itself'. Having survived the intellectual rigours of the 1980s, the concept of 'community' is now more popular than ever. So Virginia Bottomley promotes 'community care', which allows lunatics to throw themselves to the lions and Michael Howard champions 'community policing', letting the police get away with doing even less than usual. On both sides of the Atlantic, economists now worry about the limits, moral and practical, to social inequality.

In its most extreme form, the communitarian ideal rejects the modern world in favour of an idealised vision of the past. It worries about the social disintegration and personal alienation which will result from a society where, to quote RH Tawney, we are 'all elbows'. Radical communitarians, too, want to do away with selection, not to improve it; to diminish the division of labour, not to refine it; to abolish social mobility, not to accelerate it. In short, they want to re-create the organic certainties of the pre-industrial world.

It would be tempting to dismiss communitarianism of this kind as a mixture of woolly-minded thinking and political expediency. That would be to underestimate it power. Its history is one of fantastic dreams and ill-conceived policies. Harold Macmillan wanted to replace 'individualism and laissez-faire' with 'that distinct conception of society which was the distinct contribution of medieval thought'. He ended up going along with big government and nationalisation. GDH Cole wanted to replace large-scale organisations with small communes and the division of labour with voluntary association. He ended up as one of the gurus of a party committed to central planning and gigantic enterprises. The prophets of the comprehensive revolution sang the praises of the workers and their 'traditions of mutuality, qualities of emotional directness, and that intricate kaleidoscope of brass bands, humour and pigeon fancying'. They ended up condemning many bright working-class children to a life of family rows, pop culture and sullen despair.

The problem with communitarians of this ilk is their sneering hostility to the market economy and open opportunities it implies. They forget that, over the centuries, people have willingly abandoned their communities in search of higher wages and greater freedom. They also forget that the flip side of neighbourliness is bigotry. The more integrated the community, the more hostile it is likely to be to strangers and intolerant of deviants. For them, communities offer comfort only to people who are willing to stifle their wills and obey someone else's rules. There is no such thing as a free community.

Chapter 3: Meritocracy: Dream or Nightmare?

From meritocracy to dystopia

Reviving the meritocratic ideal requires us to do more than just exorcise the twin spectres of egalitarianism and radical communitarianism. It challenges us to reinvent the meritocratic ideal, bringing it up to date in a way which does not rob it of its capacity to inspire awe and imitation.

Perhaps the biggest problems for meritocrats is that so many people regard their cherished dream as a horrific nightmare. There is a long and distinguished tradition of thinking which argues that, however imperfect the world may be, a meritocracy would be even worse: a drab, cold, calculating sort of place, where the successful are intolerably smug and the unsuccessful consumed by self-loathing.

The last few years have seen the publication of a number of books — most notably Mickey Kaus's *The End of Equality*, Christopher Lasch's, *The Revolt of the Elites* and, of course, Murray and Herrnstein's *The Bell Curve* — which concentrate on the dark side of the meritocracy.

These three authors differ on some highly contentious points. Christopher Lasch argues that meritocracy is really an excuse for class interest: the so-called meritocrats are a social class, based on the control not of property but of information, and they guard their educational privileges just as jealously as the old bourgeoisie guarded their property rights. Indeed, they are rather more viscous in their pursuit of self-interest than previous ruling classes, because they think they have nobody to thank for their advantages but themselves. [14] 'The talented retain many of the vices of aristocracy without its virtues', Lasch argues. 'Their snobbery lacks any acknowledgement of reciprocal obligations between the favoured few and the multitude.'[15] Kaus worries that the United States is becoming a class society 'in the English sense', with the rich not only passing on advantages to their children, but also passing on the feeling that those advantages are deserved, the result of being not just richer but better people.[16]

For all their differences the authors all share certain worries in common, and those worries have struck a responsive chord with large numbers of readers and commentators. The books were all inspired by the widening income-gap between successful and unsuccessful Americans (a widening which has been repeated, though not quite so dramatically, in Britain.) Since 1970, the incomes of the least educated 10% have fallen; those of the modestly educated majority have stagnated; but those of the best educated 10% have surged. The effects of this have been exaggerated by the rise of the two-income household and the phenomenon known as 'assortative mating' — the tendency of high-paid lawyers to marry other high-paid lawyers. If two people earning $20,000 a year marry, their combined income is only $40,000; but if to people earning $120,000 a year marry, then their combined income is serious money. The rewards of a good education are not just a high-paying job, but a wife with a high-paying job as well.

The authors all worry that this growing inequality means that the educated no longer live in quite the same world as those over whom they hold sway. They have opted out of large parts of the public sector, swapping inner cities for suburbs, public schools for private ones and the postal service for Fedex and fax. (Robert Reich, America's labour secretary, calls this 'the secession of the successful'.) Yet they habitually make high-minded decisions about the use of public resources, introducing affirmative action and school bussing, in order to secure the just distribution of resources they themselves refuse to use.

The Bell Curve controversy

Nowhere has this debate more been more spectacularly reignited than in *The Bell Curve*, an 850 page book by Charles Murray, a social scientist already notorious for puncturing received wisdom about the welfare state, and Richard Hermnstein, a Harvard-based psychologist who died recently.

Ever since the book's publication last November IQ tests have become big news again, with pundits queuing up to expose their history, denounce their guiding assumptions and, above all, to question the motives and credentials of the surviving author, Charles Murray. Most of criticism of the book is hysterical, overblown or simply mistaken, written by people who have clearly not taken the trouble to read the book they so freely excoriate. *The Bell Curve* is, in many ways, an outstandingly piece of work, intellectually exhilarating and morally courageous. It focuses attention on a subject which academics have ignored, disparaged or wished away for a generation: individual differences in intellectual abilities. It speculates on the consequences of these differences for a world in which the returns on brains are mounting and those on brawn are diminishing and sometimes even disappearing. It points to the mounting problems that intellectually disadvantaged people face in an age of sophisticated technology, moral uncertainty and over-complex government. It suggests ways of rethinking social policy in the light of what we now know about human nature, counselling, for example, that when we try and formulate policies to lower unemployment, reduce crime or discourage welfare dependency, we must remember that the people for whom the policies are designed are often intellectually as well as socially disadvantaged.

For all these virtues, *The Bell Curve* repeatedly gives pause for doubt. The book is too insensitive to the numerous environmental factors which stop poor children from making the best of their innate abilities: at one point, for example, it argues that 'as America equalises the circumstances of people's lives, the remaining differences in intelligence are increasingly determined by differences in genes'[17], despite the fact that, as the authors themselves acknowledge in other parts of the book, America is manifestly failing to 'equalise the circumstances of people's lives'. The book is much too complacent about America's ability to make the best uses of the talents of its citizens, 'the funnelling system is already functioning to a high level of efficiency', as they put it.[18]

This underestimates both the number of gifted children who 'fall through the cracks' and end up on the scrap heap and also the number of modestly endowed people who emerge from America's PhD factories with a lucrative trade-union membership card. It is odd indeed that Murray and Herrnstein manage to be both so confident that America is turning itself into a meritocracy and yet so scathing about the damage which thirty years of egalitarianism has done to America's educational institutions.

The Bell Curve downplays the extent to which meritocracy presumes relentless and radical social mobility. Murray and Herrnstein are undoubtedly right to worry about the consequences of calcification for social cohesion and democratic politics. But they are wrong to argue that this has anything to do with the triumph of meritocracy. It has much more to do with the success of wealthy people in transmitting their privileges to their children, regardless of their individual abilities, and the reduction of opportunities for poor children to climb the educational and occupational ladder, partly thanks to educational egalitarianism.

Psychometry is a theory of social mobility not social stasis: it tries to explain why children do not always take after their parents in their intellectual abilities. The mechanism behind this relentless resorting is Mendelian inheritance, which ensures that the genes are rejigged in each generation. One expression of all this is regression to the mean: the tendency of tall parents to have slightly shorter children, for example, and for short parents to have slightly taller children. In fact, it is hereditarianism's sworn enemy, environmentalism, which is really a theory of social stasis: if the rich and educated can pass on their wealth and education to their children, unperturbed by the dance of the chromosomes, then social mobility will always be something of a freak.

Properly used, IQ tests normally promote rather than suppress social mobility. Tests are much less class-based than other forms of educational assessments such as scholastic examinations, which favour the well-taught; teachers' assessments, which favour the well-brought up; or neighbourhood schools, which institutionalise selection by house price. Tests are also much more sensitive to individual circumstances than affirmative action, which treats people, rich or poor, bright or backward, as representatives of undifferentiated social groups rather than as unique individuals. IQ tests attempt, imperfectly perhaps, but certainly better than the competition, to 'read through' the veneer of culture and reveal raw ability.

The Bell Curve is far to too sceptical about the power of social policy to equalise opportunities and promote upward mobility. Granted, heredity puts a limit to what we can make of ourselves. But it does not mean that we are all condemned to spend our lives running along the same groove. The environment plays a substantial role, never less than 20%, perhaps as much as 50%, in explaining individual differences; and raw ability can only be turned into achievements through education and training. The power of education is enormously increased if it is geared to the abilities of individual children, rather than delivered as a mass produced, wholesale, one-size-fits-all product, designed for 'the abstract child'. Many previous supporters of intelligence testing have been passionate — it is tempting to say messianic — about the capacity of education to improve the human condition.

Indeed, contrary to Murray and Herrnstein, the psychology of individual differences might well suggest a more generous, not a more parsimonious, social policy, and a more generous policy which has the added advantage of being based on the facts of human nature, not the wishes of some benevolent fantasist. The fact that some people are constitutionally dull, and therefore excluded from most of society's glittering prizes, should surely, in an enlightened society, promote a generous system of compensation. The backward should be given special education, with smaller classes and better-trained teachers than their more fortunate contemporaries; and they should be helped to find jobs, houses and a secure social niche.

Above all, *The Bell Curve* is fatally preoccupied with group differences — and particularly racial differences — in IQ. Murray and Herrnstein speculate that these differences may be genetic rather than an environmental in origin. They then argue that, if you adjust for IQ, supposed racial differences in poverty, school failure, labour participation and incarceration rates all but disappear: America is increasingly treating people according to their individual abilities (which vary, on average, between groups) rather than discriminating for or against them on the basis of their ethnic characteristics. Indeed, Murray and Herrnstein even argue that, thanks to affirmative action, blacks are 'over-represented' in white collar and professional jobs.[19]

Granted, this obsession with group differences is hard to avoid in America, not least because a succession of politicians since the 1960s, Republican as well as Democratic, have directed social policy towards groups rather than individuals. (Indeed, the practice of 'race norming', widespread on American campuses as part of their affirmative action programmes, implicitly accepts the idea that different races have different abilities by setting different pass marks for different races.) Granted, Murray and Herrnstein argue that a genetic explanation of group differences is only a hypothesis to be considered, not a dirty little secret to be exposed. But this is a road down which meritocrats should fear to tread.

For the sake of balance, it is important to emphasise that group differences in IQ may well be explicable in environmental terms. After all, blacks are, on average, poorer than whites and, again on average, have not grown up in a culture which puts overwhelming emphasis on academic achievement. Murray and Herrnstein also fail to engage in systematic international comparisons: in Britain, for example, the differences between blacks and whites is nothing like to great as it is in the United States.

This preoccupation with group differences distracts attention from the fact that IQ testing is really a science of individual, not of group differences. The differences within groups are much bigger than those between groups; and the relatively small differences between groups can easily be accounted for by social circumstances. The earliest intelligence testers were fiercely critical of a society which judged people by class, race or gender, arguing that such judgements were repugnant to the evidence of science and incompatible with the pursuit of national success. They argued that, if they were to have any chance of succeeding in an economy which depended on brain rather than brawn, nations needed to mobilise all their human resources; and the best way to do this was to ignore traditional prejudices and judge people on the basis of their personal attributes.

Murray and Herrnstein argue that, for all their paternalism, the educated are, in fact, making life more difficult for the uneducated. Their love of abstract principles, their addiction to rules, regulations and legalistic jargon, their contempt for black-and-white principles of morality, all are pushing the political and legal system in directions which the poor find confusing and alienating. The fashion for moral relativism is robbing the poor of their moral compass, and condemning them to a life of crime and illegitimacy.

Growing inequalities, they say, will not only strain the bonds of civil society beyond endurance, but will also turn America into a sort of seedy version of Brazil. The rich will live in fortified mansions on the hill; the poor will become increasingly expendable, incapable of learning any skills which will repay the 'cost of the teaching'.[20] To protect themselves, as well as increasing expenditure on law and order, the rich will create a 'custodial state', which increasingly takes over child-rearing from the poor, forces the insane into shelters, and, in general, constructs a 'high-tech and more lavish version of the Indian reservation'.[21]

This horrifying vision has provoked uproar from the left. But, in many ways, it is little more than a recapitulation of the argument at the heart of a classic of socialist polemic, written by the author of the 1945 Labour manifesto, Michael Young. In *The Rise of the Meritocracy: 1870-2033 (1959)* it was Young who first coined the term 'meritocracy', which he used in a pejorative sense to describe how horrible the world will be in 2033 if the meritocrats are allowed to seize control. They would transform equality of opportunity into an opportunity only to become unequal and promote economic efficiency at the cost of immense human misery:

> such widespread recognition of merit as the arbiter may condemn to helpless despair the many who have no merit, and do so all the more surely because the person so condemned, having too little wit to make his protest against society, may turn his anger against, and so cripple, himself.

Young was only the most intelligent of a number of communitarians who excoriated the meritocracy in the 1950s and 1960s. Many of these arguments were already familiar in conservative circles. Between the wars the most vigorous case against the meritocracy was made by cultural conservatives and intellectual elitists. TS Eliot, a self-proclaimed royalist, Anglo-Catholic and classicist, argued that meritocratic allocation would 'disorganise society and debase education'. 'We can say of Eliot', confessed Raymond Williams, a leading left wing critic, 'what Mill said of Coleridge, that 'an enlightened Radical or Liberal' ought to 'rejoice over such a Conservative'.[22]

An anatomy anatomised

Anti-meritocrats, ancient and modern, left or right, tend to advance two rather different, indeed contradictory, arguments in support of their case. The first is that meritocracy will solidify social divisions. The gap between the rich and the poor will be all the more impassable because rewards are based on the logic of biology rather than the whim of a patron or the wheel of fortune. The word which comes to mind on reading *The Bell Curve* is calcification: the authors present a picture of a society in which the distance between rich and poor is growing and mobility between the two becoming ever more uncommon. As social barriers go down, genetic barriers go up, and social divisions are inscribed in the genes, rather than shaped by social circumstances.

Yet the striking thing about biological inheritance is that it promotes social mobility, not social stasis, ensuring that many bright people have dull children, and even more dull people have bright children. Society may, indeed, be dividing into castes; but this is not because of the rise of the meritocracy but because of its opposite, the success of the middle classes in insulating themselves from meritocratic allocation. Middle-class children do so well in the educational system not because they are extraordinarily bright, but because their parents are good at finding the right schools, instilling the right values and transmitting a general respect for learning. To prevent the meritocratic ideal from degenerating into a system of class rule we need to make sure, first, that all children get a chance to master the rudiments of knowledge at as early an age as possible, and, second, that school places are allocated on the basis of objective tests, particularly IQ tests, rather than the whims of teachers.

The brings us to the other common objection to meritocracy: that it promotes relentless mobility, shredding traditions, severing social ties and stirring up discontent. John Gray has recently condemned the unfettered market for wrecking established communities and undermining inherited beliefs. We live, it seems, in an age of almost unbearable anxiety, created by the relentless drive for corporate efficiency and the entrance of low wage countries into the global economy. Surely this is no time to pile the insecurity of meritocratic selection onto the insecurity of market transactions?

In fact, this argument is hugely overstated. There is nothing like a little insecurity for sharpening the mind and strengthening the will — and nothing like security for dulling the wits or cosseting the witless. Nor is this uncertainty as unprecedented as John Gray and his fellow communitarians imply. Commentators have always been lamenting the sacrifice of established communities and ancient beliefs on the altar of profit. Karl Marx made the point particularly memorably in the *Communist Manifesto* in 1848:

> Constant revolutionising of production, uninterrupted disturbance of all social conditions, everlasting uncertainty and agitation distinguish the bourgeois epoch from all earlier ones. All fixed, fast-frozen relations, with their train of ancient and venerable prejudices and opinions are swept away, all new-formed ones become antiquated before they can ossify. All that is solid melts into air, all that is holy is profaned, and man is at last compelled to face with sober senses, his real conditions of life, and his relations with his kind.[23]

More recently, management theorists eager to spot a trend and journalists desperate to spin a story have over-estimated the extent to which corporations are shedding staff and introducing short-term contracts. The average length of time spent working for a company is much as it has been since the Second World War, about ten years.

Far from being a solvent of communities, meritocracy requires communities in order to function. The building blocks of the meritocracy are successful schools and colleges, and successful schools and colleges are, among other things, flourishing communities, laboriously created over many generations to transform raw abilities into useable talents. The best schools are successful precisely because they have a strong sense of collective identity, drawn from proud traditions, reinforced by collective rituals and dedicated to a common purpose, and because they are determined to impose that identity upon their pupils, regardless of the temptations of popular custom and passing fashions.

Meritocratic selection also creates communities where none might have existed. Throw people of vastly different abilities together and they will soon tire of each other. Throw like-minded people together, however, and they will quickly coalesce into communities. Oxford colleges choose people from different backgrounds, social and geographical, but with broadly similar abilities and encourage them to live together for a few years. The result is a collection of extraordinary vibrant communities, as people who might have spent their lives as misfits discover that their is some point in talking to their fellow eighteen year-olds.

A third objection to meritocracy is that it inevitably produces a permanent underclass. Lacking the one thing which makes for success, the dim sink to the bottom of society; lacking any sense of self-worth, they vent their frustration on themselves, their families and any strangers who have the misfortune to meet them. In fact, any civilised meritocracy will judge itself by the success with which it deals with its less able members. Because it makes full use of its human resources, a meritocracy has the resources to look after the unfortunate; and because it develops ways of distinguishing between the backward and the lazy, a meritocracy allows welfare payments to be concentrated on the truly deserving. The fact that some people are dull through no fault of their own — because of their genes rather than their character — dispels notions of blame and penny-pinching. Instead, it should promote a generous system of compensation, since the dull are excluded, through no fault of their own, from society's glittering prizes. The backward are given special education, with smaller classes and better-trained teachers than their more fortunate contemporaries; and then helped to find jobs, houses and a secure social niche.

Taking talents seriously

In the last thirty years respectable academic opinion has turned against the two ideas which lie at the foundation of a meritocratic society: that individuals differ in their natural talents and that the best way to make the most of these talents is to provide equality of opportunity. Some egalitarians have argued that talents are not really 'natural'; others that rewarding people for being bright amounts to nothing more than rewarding them for being the winners of a lottery. On the contrary, there is a strong moral case for taxing the bright to compensate the dull for their bad luck.

At the opposite end of the political spectrum, libertarians have argued that equality of opportunity is nothing more than a dangerous chimera. The best way to enforce it would be to nationalise childrearing, raising all children in state nurseries; and even less drastic methods involve unacceptable interference in personal freedom. Besides, from the libertarian perspective, there is no such thing as a natural talent, perpetually worthy of special reward:

the market constantly shifts the value which it places on individuals and their activities.

These criticisms rest on sharply different assumptions about the facts of genetics and the moral claims of the state. But their cumulative effect has been to weaken meritocracy as a political force and to allow egalitarians to seize the initiative and destroy an educational system based on the idea that children should be sorted and educated according to their differing talents.

The timing of this anti-meritocratic fashion is exceedingly odd. It has coincided with a flurry of scientific studies which make it fairly clear that differences in intelligences are substantially inherited. The Minnesota twin study in 1990 — the largest and most sophisticated of its kind ever attempted — demonstrated that identical twins separated at birth have remarkably similar IQs. It has also coincided with a shift, in the advanced world, from a manufacturing to an information-based economy. The prosperity of advanced countries increasingly depends on their ability to identify, nurture and promote talent — particularly exceptional talent. Yet, at the same time, intellectuals slight the idea that individuals differ in talents and policy-makers reject the idea that the educational system is, among other things, a giant capacity-catching machine. It is rather as if, having learned that coal is our only source of power, the government decided to close the coal mines and re-employ all coal-miners as ballroom dancers.

The abundance of scientific evidence about the hereditability of intelligence does not obviate the need for hard work. Turning an ability into a talent is far from easy: it requires self-denial (we must train when we would rather be relaxing), investment (we must spend time and money cultivating our abilities), and risk-taking (a talent may wear out, lose market value or fail to materialise: after years of effort, we may find that we are simply not up to scratch). Above average rewards thus induce people to create talents and reward them for the self-sacrifice which that creation entails.

The strongest argument for taking talents seriously, however, is not one of efficiency but of morality. What distinguishes us as human beings is the fact that we possess talents, intellectual, artistic, moral or whatever. By encouraging people to discover and develop their talents, we encourage them to discover and develop their moral selves. By evaluating people on the basis of those talents, we demonstrate that we are taking them seriously as self-governing individuals, who are capable of dreaming their dreams and willing their fates. We cannot respect people unless we take talents seriously.

Those free-marketeers who dismiss equality of opportunity underestimate its importance for legitimising the market economy, and making full-use of the talents of the population. The inequalities which increasingly characterise market economies are hard to justify if some sections of the population feel that they have been excluded from the chance to better themselves, on account of irrelevancies such as their race, sex or background, or if they believe that the rules have been bent against them.

Free-marketeers also overestimate the difficulty of providing something approximating to equal opportunities. Equality of opportunity is not such a demanding goal as some libertarians imagine. It does not mean ensuring that everybody starts from exactly the same point. That would be impossible without huge restrictions on personal freedom. It does not even mean spending the same amount on each child's education. James Coleman has demonstrated that equalising educational resources does not abolish the influence of social class from the classroom. Instead, it means ensuring that everybody has a chance of taking part in the race for success. In education, this means, at the very least, ensuring that everybody can read, write and count as early and easily as possible. That may well involve providing underprivileged children (particularly children from broken homes) with compensatory education, starting with high-quality nursery schools, and with state subsidies to stop them from dropping out of school earlier than their equally talented but richer contemporaries. It will certainly mean ensuring that everybody is judged according to the objective standards, preferably through frequent examinations. Two aspects of this system require further examination: competition and selection.

Chapter 4: Competition and Selection

Only compete

A crucial component of equality of opportunity is frequent educational competitions, in the form of scholarships, prizes and public examinations. As my colleague at All Souls, Simon Green, has pointed out, competitions reveal otherwise unknown information about the relative abilities of those who take part in them.[24] They provide educators with information about people's suitability for further education, and society with information about people's ability to hold important jobs. In doing so they also provide about the best way of distributing scarce resources both efficiently and justly.

Another important component is educational selection. Selection has long been anathema to the educational establishment. But the case against introducing a little more rigour into the current educational lottery owes more to sentiment than logic. The range of abilities and aptitudes in the population is so wide, the variety of demands which a sophisticated economy imposes on its citizens so diverse, the case for social mobility so compelling, that secondary schools need to be much more choosy about their pupils.

Selective schools are more effective than non-selective schools, since they can impose their collective characters on their pupils much more effectively than schools which are forced to take all and sundry. They pursue clear goals, establish firm objectives, elaborate appropriate methods for achieving those objectives, and introduce appropriate incentives and punishments on their pupils, including, at the extreme, expulsion. They impose their corporate identities on their pupils, demanding that they identify with the school rather than with their peer group and that they spend their time internalising the values of all that is best in adult culture. These schools teach pupils who possess similar abilities and aspirations, so that teachers can be sure that they are pitching their teaching at the right level and pupils can compete on a rough level of equality. Above all, they institutionalise competition, channelling adolescent competitiveness into academic achievement rather than allowing it to be dissipated on the fripperies of youth culture, and ensuring that pupils perform as near as possible to their full potential.

Building a new consensus

Taking meritocracy seriously requires a revolution in the thinking of all Britain's political parties. They would have to agree that the fundamental aim of the government is to enable people to fulfil their innate abilities, however high that takes them, and that, apart from defence and law and order, the most important function of the state is the education of its citizens. Reaching such a consensus for meritocracy poses fundamental challenges to the way established parties think and also about the way in which the voters perceive them.

The right has travelled furthest in the meritocratic direction — not least because it had furthest to travel. For much of this century Conservatives have suffered from a debilitating weakness for blue blood and strangulated accents. Bonar Law's Cabinet including eight aristocrats, both Baldwin's cabinets nine, and Chamberlain's eight. All this began to change in the mid-1960s, after the fourteenth Mr Wilson defeated the fourteenth Earl of Hume. The last three leaders of the Conservative Party have all been grammar school educated (though Edward Heath did his best to play the part of a product of some minor public school.)

The most important of these, in meritocratic terms, was Margaret Thatcher. She did more than any of her predecessors to force her party to come to terms with modernity. Her Cabinet was more Old Estonian than Old Etonian, as Lord Carrington famously remarked, and some of her favourite colleagues, like David Young and Norman Tebbit, were obvious new men. Her government fell out with just about every bit of the old establishment: the BBC, the BMA, the bishops, the barristers, even the Monarchy. Her enthusiasm for exposing the City and industry to market forces helped to shift power from the nice-but-dims to the sharp-but-dynamic. John Major has tried to continue in the same establishment-busting vain, refining the internal market in health and education, introducing performance contracts for senior civil servants and extending contracting out and market testing throughout the lower civil service.

But the right remains hopelessly compromised by its addiction to the ancient constitution and its habit of pampering Britain's already pampered business elites. It has stubbornly refused to start thinking seriously about the Monarchy and the House of Lords. It lamentably failed to realise, in privatising utilities like water and gas, that regulation is no substitute for competition. Worse still, the right is distinctly nervous about those areas of the public sector where it has applied a modicum of competition, notably the health service and education.

More vigorous support for meritocracy would give the right a coherent agenda. Mrs Thatcher used the market to transform conservatism from a defence of inherited privilege into a solvent of vested interests. The task now facing the right is to use the concept of merit to complete and civilise this revolution, extending the competitive principle from the public to the private sector but, at the same time, making sure that everybody, regardless of parental wealth or family connections, has a chance to get ahead. The last fifteen years will have been a terrible failure if those who prospered under Mrs Thatcher are allowed to pull the ladder up behind them.

Meritocracy also poses a challenge to the left and provides a true test as to whether it has broken with its old ways of thinking. Traditionally the debate about whether the left has come to terms with modernity has always turned on its attitude to the market. Has it finally kicked its intervention-and-subsidy habit? Does it realise that the price-mechanism can be used to invigorate the public as well as the private sector? And is it prepared for the downside as well as the up-swing of Schumpeter's awe-inspiring cycle of 'creative destruction'? The left's attitude to meritocracy is almost as vital as its stance on the workings of a modern economy.

For decades the left has been sharply divided between meritocrats and communitarians. The meritocratic ideal played a central role in establishing the left as a serious political force by weaving three powerful intellectual traditions into a more or less coherent ideology: the Enlightenment commitment to reason and opportunity; the Liberal hostility to patronage, corruption and other dodges designed to support the luxuries of the rich at the expense of the labours of the poor; and the Nonconformist belief in the spiritual elect. Throughout the first half of the century this ideal served the left well. Meritocracy allowed it to be both reforming and responsible, worried about inequality but keen on economic efficiency.

'New' Labour would like to retake this ground, but the legacy bequeathed by communitarians since they seized control in the 1960s will prove difficult to overturn. Even as it comes to terms, albeit reluctantly, with grant-maintained schools and pupil-related funding, it is embracing affirmative action by introducing women-only short lists in the selection of some of its parliamentary candidates.

Powerful interest groups within the left remain anti-meritocrats to their fingertips. Trade unions are as vigorous as ever in opposing meritocratic management methods, ranging from performance-related pay to flexible contracts, and are likely to get more vigorous still as the European Union reinforces their position with various legal and constitutional rights. The lumpen polytechnic, that vast mass of civil servants, social workers, local government officers, college lecturers and BBC journalists who set the moral tone of the country, are equally vehement in their opposition regarding meritocracy is a feeble creed, sociologically naive and emotionally repugnant.

Re-establishing a political consensus for meritocracy is possible but it is far from easy. The temptation to side with the communitarians is much greater since it allows politicians to capitalise on a national love affair with community. But the price of this strategy will be ruinous: it will mean backing the forces of conservatism and inertia which are blind to the problems plaguing the unreformed welfare state, indebted to vested interests in the public sector, and bent on restoring Britain to a golden age that never was.

Chapter 5: Rebuilding Education

Meritocracy starts here

Anyone who wants to rebuild meritocracy must start by rebuilding education. The revolt against the meritocracy led to an educational revolution which may well have done more long-term harm to our competitiveness than even the most misguided attempts at intervention and subsidy. The revolt did not just result in the destruction of the grammar schools. It also determined the character of the comprehensives and the nature of primary, and even infant schools. Having got rid of selection, egalitarians insisted on getting rid of streaming as well; having got rid of streaming, they insisted on introducing informal teaching methods. Comprehensives were to be 'equality machines', with mixed-ability classes and an unstructured, 'pally' style of teaching, devoted to the building of self-esteem rather than the transmission of knowledge.

All this started with the introduction of the comprehensives, and it is with the reform of the comprehensives that we must start if we want to reverse the tide. Though the right is fond of teasing the left for praising comprehensives in theory while fleeing them in practice, its own recent educational policy has been far from coherent. The government makes it clear that it has no desire to see a wholesale reintroduction of selection. Grant-maintained schools are only allowed to select a certain proportion of their pupils and City Technology Colleges are forced to take their pupils from the entire ability range.

This ambivalence about comprehensives is far from new. Mrs Thatcher sanctioned the destruction of more grammar schools than any Labour minister; Lord Joseph completed the comprehensive revolution by replacing O-levels and CSEs with GCSEs; and Kenneth Baker imposed a national curriculum which was a monument to the hubris of bureaucrats and the continuing influence of progressive theorists. The result was a syllabus which bored the able, confused the dull and alienated the teaching profession.

The right is nervous about the full-scale reintroduction of selection because so many middle-class parents, particularly in the suburbs, are happy with the neighbourhood principle, which guarantees even their dullest children a place in an acceptable school. When the Conservative-controlled council tried to bring back formal academic selection in Solihull, Birmingham, in the early 1980s, their middle-class constituents revolted, arguing that, in buying expensive houses, they had effectively bought places in good schools, and they would not tolerate working-class children taking those places just because they happened to be good at passing exams.

Fortunately, there has been more to recent educational policy than this sort of suburban turf protection. Though she was initially outmanoeuvred by educational bureaucrats, Mrs Thatcher identified comprehensives with equality and equality with national humiliation. Right-wing meritocrats who broke with the left over the question of grammar schools conducted a long campaign to persuade the Party leadership to take education more seriously, and this finally resulted in a far-reaching, if flawed, piece of legislation, the 1988 Education Act.

A new market in merit

The Act created new sorts of schools outside local education authority control: City Technology Colleges, which received some of their funding from industry as well as the state and which were free to concentrate on vocational subjects and teach for longer than the normal school day; and Grant Maintained Schools, which are funded directly by central government and are free to specialise in certain subjects and cultivate their own teaching styles. The Act also gave all schools, including those which stayed under their local education authorities, more control over their own budgets. The aim of all this was as much pedagogical as financial. What makes schools successful is their ethos. But outside bureaucrats habitually destroy this ethos in their enthusiasm for fitting schools into national systems and subjecting them to central rules: opting out of bureaucratic control is a precondition for opting into excellence.

The Act also linked schools' incomes to the number of pupils they attract. More recently, the government has provided parents with the information they need to make informed choices, through league tables of academic results and truancy rates. The watchwords of the emerging system are competition, schools vying with each other for pupils and going out of business if they fail to attract enough pupils, and consumer power, effectively turning each child into an educational voucher by making him free to move to any school which will have him. The government hopes that this internal market will produce the benefits of higher standards without the pain of educational selection. Competition will force all schools to get better, while the creation of a wide variety of different kinds of schools will help match opportunities to aptitudes.

In fact, of course, the internal market is forcing educational selection back onto the agenda. Schools are much happier selecting pupils than expanding indefinitely. Selection allow schools to boost their place in league tables by recruiting the brightest pupils — thus guaranteeing them an even longer queue of would-be pupils in the future. Besides, there are severe practical problems to expansion. The pupil-related funding formula does not take into account the expense of building new classrooms. More importantly, good schools cannot go on expanding for ever without sacrificing the very thing which makes them good in the first place. Moreover, giving schools more freedom from central control does not amount to much if they are not able to influence the nature of their intake.

The question at the heart of the educational debate is not whether to select, but how. Schools are currently selecting by fairly crude and impressionistic methods. Geography — does the child live near the school? Family connections — does he have a sibling at the school? Good breeding — does he behave well at interviews? Parental status — is his father leader of a major political party? The first two of these are just the comprehensive principle writ large. There is no point in introducing open enrolment if children continue to go to their local schools. The second two raise the spectre of class prejudice. Teachers are notoriously inclined to favour middle-class children in interviews. Selection based on academic records favours the well-taught rather than the innately able. There is a serious danger, then, that the current system of parental choice will be little more than an excuse for the pushy middle-classes to elbow the workers out of the way.

To guard against this schools need to make sure that they are selecting people on the basis of promise not just achievement. Schools which select on the basis of innate ability will recruit children from all social classes. They will also get much better academic results, because they recruit talent from the whole of society rather than just a narrow stratum. The best schools will be those which adopt the most objective method for selecting their pupils. In other words, schools need to start using IQ tests again.

The late 11-plus raises many ghosts, though it was by no means as ghoulish as many commentators have claimed; indeed, its abolition consigned many bright working-class children to a life of frustrated ambitions and unfulfilled talents. But there was nevertheless a good deal wrong with the system: the shortage of grammar-school places in the more populous and prosperous south-east, the once-and-for all nature of classification, and, above all, the shortage of technical schools for non-academic children.

Policy-makers must ensure that these problems are not recreated. The best way to do this is to make sure that the million or so spare school places are treated as an opportunity to be seized rather than a problem to be tidied away, as the Department for Education would prefer. The spare places should be used to ensure that demand is not frustrated by supply. They should also be used to ensure that there are many different kinds of schools, suitable for the huge variety of human talents. Voluntary groups, local businesses, religious organisations, all should be allowed to bid for surplus school buildings and set up schools (provided, of course, they teach core disciplines and comply with all reasonable regulations). Local authorities should also consider breaking the monster comprehensives of the 1960s into separate schools, sharing the same buildings but each developing a distinct ethos.

The multiplication of types of schools could go some way to reducing the problem of selection. Provided that there are plenty of different sorts of schools children with different sorts of aptitudes will discover appropriate niches: self-allocation will replace academic selection. It should ensure that selection is provisional and reversible rather than definitive and final. Above all, it should also ensure that there is a flourishing vocational school system for children whose talents and inclinations do not fit into an academic mould.

To complete this revolution in the character of schools the Department for Education should make much more use of prizes and scholarships. So much use, in fact, that money is increasingly linked to performance rather than doled out as an entitlement. Successful schools could receive bonuses from the Department for Education. Careful use of examination results and IQ tests could ensure that these bonuses rewarded value added, so that teachers were not simply rewarded for having clever pupils. The Department should pay substantial prizes for outstanding performance in examinations at 11, 14, 16 and 18. It should also create national merit scholarships to support outstanding students while they are at university or pay off their debts if they get a First. Such prizes will not only provide a proper reward for excellence; they will also spread an ethos of effort and achievement throughout the educational system, since even children who fail to win prizes profit from having taken part in the competition.

The new school tie

It is futile to dream of a more meritocratic Britain without confronting the hoary problem of the public schools. Generations of meritocrats have looked at the way those schools give the British class system a peculiarly sharp edge, consolidating inherited privileges and segregating the ruling class from the mass of the population, and have called for their abolition. They are right to worry, but wrong to call for abolition, which would be both an intolerable intrusion into personal freedom and a cowardly way of dodging the real issue: why people, not all of them disgustingly rich, are determined to opt out of the state sector.

Thankfully, there are more imaginative ways of dealing with the problem. Reinvigorating the grammar schools is one. The grammar schools have always given the public schools a run for their money; indeed, in the wake of the second world war, many people predicted that public schools would soon be defunct as grammar schools took over the function of educating the nation's elite. Since the abolition of the grammar schools Oxford and Cambridge have had to resort to ever more desperate types of affirmative action, culminating in the abolition of traditional college entrance exams, to ensure that as many as half of their places go to state schools. But we can do something even better than just improving the state sector. We can abolish the divisions between the two sectors completely, making it possible for everybody in the country, however slender their means, to send their children to private schools.

There are two possible ways of doing this: by using the state power in more imaginative ways, or by handing power back over to parents.

The Department for Education could start thinking of itself as a purchasing agent, charged with securing the best education for children, rather than as a bureaucratic patron, obsessed with creating jobs for state-certified teachers. It should welcome great schools like Manchester Grammar School, which were driven into the private sector by egalitarian dogmatism, back into the public sector. It should also purchase a certain number of places in the best public schools, organising an annual examination to make sure that those places are awarded to the brightest children in the country, however poor their parents. The public schools, mindful of their charitable status, their exemption from VAT and the advantages of bulk purchasing, will no doubt be willing to sell places to the government at a generous discount. This will mean that every child in the country will have a chance of attending a public school. It will also mean that public schools will no longer occupy a segregated enclave but will instead straddle the public-private divide, taking some fee paying children and some state scholarship winners.

Policy-makers should also think seriously about issuing parents with vouchers, which they can use in schools of their choice, private or public, and which they are free to top-up with their own money. The case has been raised and dismissed so often that one almost hesitates to raise it again, for fear of being considered a bore. But opponents of vouchers have usually relied on prejudice and nit-picking rather than principle and broad-ranging argument. The Treasury worries about the 'deadweight' cost of vouchers (because parents who opt out of the state system will no longer have to pay twice for their children's education.) The government argues that we already have a 'virtual' voucher system, thanks to open enrolment and pupil-related funding, ignoring the fact that today's vouchers can only be spent in government-managed outlets.

Behind all of these objections is the fear that vouchers will exacerbate Britain's social divisions. People who habitually send their children to Eton or Winchester will find themselves £2,500 a year richer, courtesy of the state. The aspiring middle classes will flee the state system entirely. The only people left in the state system will be the poor, the dull and the terminally unambitious. The flight of the middle classes will produce a dismal cycle, as the exit of the educated reduces pressure for better state schools and deteriorating state schools encourage yet more of the educated to leave.

In fact, vouchers are remarkably effective ways of helping the poor because they can be adjusted to take into account the particular circumstances of real people rather than the presumed needs of vaguely defined groups. The size of the voucher can be inversely linked to income, so that poorer people get much more to spend on education. The state can also encourage people to make the best use of these extra resources by setting up 'educational advice bureaux', scattered throughout poorer areas, which provide detailed information about the performance of local schools. Whenever the state has tried to promote equality by funding institutions it has ended up by reinforcing middle-class advantages; by shifting resources from institutions to individuals it has a real chance of breaking the lamentable link between poverty and educational failure.

A full-voucher scheme will have two further advantages. By allowing parents to top-up vouchers from their own pockets it will increase the amount of money spent on education. Today parents face a stark choice between spending £10,000 a year educating their children or sending them to a 'free' state school. The Treasury effectively sets a limit on the amount that most people can spend on schooling. Vouchers will allow parents to add anything from a few hundred to a few thousand pounds to the amount they spend on education. This will give parents much more control over their discretionary income. It will also raise the amount of money which society as a whole invests in human capital. Above all, vouchers will deliver the killer blow to educational apartheid. Instead of an educational system sharply divided into two sorts of schools, one wholly fee paying, one wholly state supported, Britain will generate a richly variegated system, with different schools drawing different proportions of their incomes from public grants and private contributions.

Nursing the meritocracy

Building a meritocracy will necessitate investing more money on one particular aspect of education: nursery schools — especially nursery schools attended by the socially disadvantaged. To provide equality of opportunity, Britain must ensure that all children have a reasonable chance of acquiring basic skills; to make full use of its human resources Britain must compensate for the poor environments of its most unfortunate members. After all, the outcome of a competitive education system can hardly be regarded as just if some competitors start off far behind their competitors, and weighed down by balls and chains.

Nursery schools can provide parents with vital support during some of the most difficult years of child-rearing. They can offer unfortunate children the stability and stimulation they fail to get at home. They can also contribute far more to the battle against crime than any number of 'short sharp shocks' or prison building programmes. Yet Britain, with more working mothers and broken families than other West European countries, offers publicly-financed nursery education to fewer than 50% of its 3-5 year-olds, compared with 77% in Germany, 85% in Denmark and Italy, and 95% in France.

There are three commonly-heard objections to publicly-funded pre-school education. The first, from the right, is that it is tantamount to nationalising child-rearing and extending the low standards of state primary schools to private nursery schools. This can be easily dealt with by offering vouchers for nursery school education, which can be redeemed in the private as well as the public sector. The second, from the Treasury, is that this represents a subsidy to the middle classes, who already pay for their children to go to nursery schools. This could be dealt with by inversely linking the value of the vouchers to parental incomes. The third and most persuasive objection is that there are always good arguments for spending public money and it is giving into too many of them that has got the country into its current predicament. In fact, the money for the nursery schools could come from another part of the educational budget, the universities. The government currently pays all university students' fees and the bulk of his or her living expenses. This is not only regressive, because students are mainly middle-class by social origin and overwhelmingly middle-class by social destination, and restrictive, since the number of students is limited by Treasury fiat rather than demand; it is also absurdly generous for a middle-ranking European country, committing Britain to spending more public money per student than almost any country in the world.

The universities should be allowed to charge fees to their students. The State should switch completely from grants to loans. Students could be free to pay for their education up-front, at a discount. National scholarship winners would also get their university educations 'free'. But most would rely on state loans to cover fees and maintenance, repayable as jobs and incomes allow. The loans could be gathered through the National Insurance System, but they would not be in the form of a tax, because ex-students would stop paying once they had covered the cost of their education. Pioneered in Australia, this system frees dons from bureaucratic interference, allows universities to expand and, at the same time, ensures that those who reap the bulk of the benefits of benefits of higher education bear most of the costs.

Primary problems

Providing more nursery schools will be fairly pointless unless we inject a little more rigour into primary education. English primary schools are remarkably nice places: children sit around in groups (rows of desks have long been forbidden) expressing their views and preparing their projects. On the floors lie toys and exciting looking engines; the walls are decorated with brightly coloured pictures. From time to time a teacher will interrupt their discussions to ask a question or — if she is a strict disciplinarian — offer an opinion.

Alas, niceness is not enough. For decades this amiable anarchy has failed to instil knowledge and discipline. The immense capacity of young children to absorb knowledge has been wasted, and children leave their primary schools less prepared for advanced learning than their rivals in most other major countries. It is all very pleasant. But it is not education.

The niceness revolution is a legacy of the 1960s. The Plowden report turned progressive child-centred education from a minority fad (practised mainly in private schools patronised by the progressive intelligentsia) into an entrenched orthodoxy. The most sacred tenet in this orthodoxy is learning by experience. The teacher presents children with a topic and allows them to approach it in any way that takes their fancy. There is no sense that knowledge is divided into specific subjects and that effort is required to master those subjects. The most important thing is that the child should initiate the whole process. The basics are taught indirectly — if at all. Literacy and numeracy are the by-products of a project which is initiated by the child, involves as little stress as possible, and is anchored in every day experience.

This might have been admirable if project-work had remained an enjoyable side-line to traditional teaching. But it became the be-all and end-all of classroom teaching. The only acceptable way to teach skills was to weave them into experience. Anyone who questioned this orthodoxy was told that they do not understand 'good primary practice'. Children have paid a high price for this cheerful orthodoxy. Their education has been retarded for at least a couple of years: primary schools have come to resemble old-fashioned nursery schools and the first forms of secondary schools turned into old-fashioned primary schools. Children routinely fail to learn the basic rules of spelling or to master such short-cuts to mental arithmetic as the multiplication tables. The loss of knowledge has not necessarily been compensated with an increase in happiness. Given an open-ended brief to pursue their interests, they have little sense of goals and objectives. The initial delight in freedom usually gives way to confusion and anomie.

Nor is progressivism as innocent as it might look at first glance. The progressive classroom was a laboratory of the classless society — an idyllic place in which co-operation flourished and competition was unknown. Nothing angers the progressive teachers quite so much as testing, which, they argue, measures little more than social background and so simply perpetuates and justifies social inequalities. Children who are labelled as failures at primary school are likely to go on to fulfil their own low expectations. The yobs on the football terraces were venting their anger at those nasty spelling tests.

The paradox of Plowdenism is that it has reinforced the social divisions it was meant to challenge. Poor children find it much more difficult to adjust to the unstructured environment of progressive schools than their middle-class contemporaries. Middle-class parents make up for the failure of schools to impart basic knowledge: working-class parents assume (not unreasonably) that school teachers were doing what they were paid for.

The 1988 Education Act was intended to introduce a little rigour into primary schools: a core curriculum would give them a mission; regular examinations at seven and 11 would measure whether the curriculum was being delivered; and pupil-driven funding would ensure that good schools flourished and bad schools improved — or died. But there are already signs that new methods are being used to perpetuate old purposes, codifying progressivism rather than supplanting it. The new tests have been invented by educational bodies steeped in the old educational orthodoxy. They are intended to register processes rather than measure achievements. Instead of simply asking teachers to find out whether children can do simple sums and spell basic words, the authorities insist that they analyse the learning processes involved.

From dependency to self-help

Thinking again about the structure of British education should be part of a much broader exercise in thinking again about the nature of the British welfare state. Invented to serve an economic and moral order which has long since vanished, the welfare state is becoming an obstacle to spreading meritocratic values among a significant section of the British population. Beveridge assumed that unemployment was a matter of idling, hopefully for just a few weeks, between one low skilled job and another. Today, low skilled jobs are disappearing, destroyed by machines or exported to the third world, and the most pressing need is not for handouts to tide people over, but for training to make them employable in a more demanding labour market. Beveridge assumed that people would wait until they had got married and become self-supporting before having children. In fact, in most inner-cities a third of children are born to unmarried mothers and profligate fathers. People treat welfare payments as rights which impose no obligations on them to change their behaviour or improve their market value. Beveridge assumed that bureaucrats would do their best to help their clients and that the clients would do their best to become self-supporting. In fact, many bureaucrats are concerned with making their own lives easier, and many of their clients are content to become permanent wards of the state. Preserving the Beveridgian structure in a world where stable manual jobs have disappeared and the old-fashioned culture of self-improvement has imploded is proving to be a disaster, both financially and morally.

The poorest Britons are being inculcated with values which will prevent them from becoming active citizens of a meritocracy. Policy-makers must ensure that people cannot languish on the dole without undergoing education and training. They must remove the perverse incentives which reward mothers for having children out of wedlock (with council flats, for example) and punish them for getting married (with reduced child-care payments). They must channel as much money as possible to children rather than to adults.

We need to replace the welfare state with the opportunity state. Universal nursery school education could ensure that everybody has a foot on the first rung of the educational ladder (and, incidentally, make the lives of mothers a little more tolerable). Educational vouchers could be used to direct more resources to poor families and make public schools available to all. Scholarships and bursaries could be used to ensure that underprivileged children stay on in the sixth form and go to university.

Chapter 6: Conclusion

We should not delude ourselves into thinking that reviving the meritocracy will be easy. Who will be its voice in Parliament? The left has a record of destroying grammar schools, protecting collective bargaining and falling in love with group rights. It is also too inclined to think that the solution to any problem lies in spending more money, rather than reforming managerial structures. The right is growing soft on vested interests, and is too inclined to ascribe our current constitutional arrangements to eternal wisdom. Who will lead its revival in academia? The anti-meritocrats, who captured so many university departments in the 1960s, are being reinforced, thanks to the fashion for post-structuralism, gender studies and 'social balance', by ever more extreme exponents of group thinking and affirmative action. That most saccharine of words, 'community', continues to exercise a wide appeal: listen to 'thought for the day' on any morning of the week, or turn to the op-ed columns of the quality newspapers.

So why bother? Why rush ahead with yet another upheaval in British life? The British, it is said, have had enough of ideological rule and legislative hyperactivity. The cry is for an end to strife, a break from upheavals, a return of civilised pragmatism. The trouble is that the status quo isn't tenable: the world is not going to stop turning for a few years, while the British take a nap. Everywhere governments have realised that, in an age of lightning capital flows and globe-spanning corporations, their best chance for prosperity lies in streamlining government and improving education. Only by educating their workforces can countries attract the world's high value-added jobs. Only by educating their workforces can countries master technological upheaval and corporate restructuring. And only by streamlining their government can countries provide social services without imposing intolerable taxes on companies and citizens.

Governments everywhere are reforming education, improving the teaching of basic subjects, expanding their universities, strengthening their training systems.[25] The Germans are determined to refine an apprenticeship system which has long been the envy of the world. The French are committed to improving the education of middle-ability students. Having mastered mass production, the south-east Asians are determined to break the West's stranglehold on high value-added jobs. In Hong Kong, doctors complain that children are carrying so many books home in the evenings that they risk spinal curvature. In South Korea, even the dustiest back street contains some private school or academy. In Japan, children leave their state schools at the end of a working day only to spend their evenings sitting in cramming schools. In Singapore, the government has created one of the greatest capacity-catching machines the world has ever seen.

The choice is between reviving meritocracy and acquiescing in decline. Sitting still is no longer an option.

Notes & References

[1] Francis Fukuyama, 'The Future of Equality', The National Interest, Winter, 1994-5, p.97

[2] Noel Annan, 'The Intellectual Aristocracy', in JH Plumb (ed.), *Studies in Social History. A Tribute to GM Trevelyan* (1955), pp.241-287. I have discussed the rise and fall of meritocracy in greater detail in *Measuring the Mind. Education and Psychology in England c.1860-1990* (CUP, 1994). See pp.164-340.

[3] Macaulay Report on the Indian Civil Service, November, 1854. As reprinted in *Report of the Committee on the Civil Service, 1966-68* (Cmnd 3638, chairman Lord Fulton), Vol. 1, appendix B, p.122.

[4] John Stuart Mill, Reform of the Civil Service, Essays on Politics and Society, *Collected Works of John Stuart Mill*, XVIII, p.207. Originally printed in 'Papers relating to the Re-organisation of the Civil Service', Parliamentary Papers, 1854-55, XX, pp.92-8. For the circumstances surrounding Mill's paper see the textual introduction, p.lxxx.

[5] See, for example, Colin Lacey, *Hightown Grammar. The School as a Social System* (Manchester, 1970), pp. 26-31 and fig. 3, p.14. See also Eric James, Education and Leadership (1951).

[6] G Orwell, *The Road to Wigan Pier* (Harmondsworth, 1962 ed), p.108.

[7] FW Farrar, 'Public School Education', *Fortnightly Review*, 3 (March, 1868), pp.239-40.

[8] CAR Crosland, *The Future of Socialism* (1956), p.258; c.f. with *Socialism Now* (1974), pp.194-5.

[9] *ibid.*, p.235. Crosland acknowledged that his views on this point owed much to discussions with Michael Young.

[10] Brian Jackson, *Streaming* (1964), p.141.

[11] Christopher Jencks (and Marshall Smith, Henry Acland, Mary Jo Bane, David Cohen, Herbert Gintis, Barbara Heyns, Stephen Michelson), Inequality. A Reassessment of the Effect of Family of Schooling in America (New York, 1972).

[12] AH Halsey (ed.), *Department of Education and Science, Educational Priority*, Volume 1, Problems and Policies (HMSO 1972), p.6. Cf. Halsey, 'Sociology and the Equality Debate', *Oxford Review of Education*, Vol. 1 (Oxford, 1975), pp. 9-26.

13 This was one of the main themes of post-War sociology. For convenient summaries of the literature see, Julian Le Grand, *The Strategy of Equality: Redistribution and the Social Services* (London, 1982) and Robert E. Goodin and Julian Le Grand, *Not Only the Poor: The Middle Classes and the Welfare State* (London, 1987).

14 Christopher Lasch, *The Revolt of the Elites* (1995), p.39

15 *ibid.*, p.45

16 Kaus, *The End of Equality*, p.17

17 Richard Herrnstein and Charles Murray, 'The Bell Curve. Intelligence and Class Structure in American Life' New York, 1994), p.91

18 *ibid.*, p.114

19 *ibid.*, p.479

20 *ibid.*, p.526

21 *ibid.*, p.526

22 Raymond Williams, *Culture and Society 1780-1950* (1959), p.227.

23 Karl Marx and Frederick Engels, Manifesto of the Communist Party (1848). Reprinted in Karl Marx, *The Revolutions of 1848* edited and introduced by David Fernbach (Harmondsworth, 1973), pp. 70-1.

24 SJD Green, 'Competitive Equality of Opportunity: a defence', *Ethics* , vol. 100, no. 1, October 1989, pp.5-32.

25 I have discussed this theme in more detail in 'Coming Top: A Survey of Education', *Economist*, 21 Nov 1992.

PAPERS IN PRINT   Price

REPORTS

OCCASIONAL PAPERS

OTHER PAPERS

MEMORANDA

HARD DATA